Twin Peaks

Quilts from Easy Strip-Pieced Triangles

Twin Peaks

Quilts from Easy Strip-Pieced Triangles

Gayle Bong

Twin Peaks:
Quilts from Easy Strip-Pieced Triangles
© 2008 by Gayle Bong

That Patchwork Place® is an imprint of
Martingale & Company®.

Martingale & Company
20205 144th Ave. NE
Woodinville, WA 98072-8478 USA
www.martingale-pub.com

Printed in China
13 12 11 10 09 08 8 7 6 5 4 3 2 1

Library of Congress Cataloging-in-Publication Data
Library of Congress Control Number: 2008033550

ISBN: 978-1-56477-834-5

Mission Statement

*Dedicated to providing quality products and
service to inspire creativity.*

CREDITS

President & CEO: Tom Wierzbicki
Editorial Director: Mary V. Green
Managing Editor: Tina Cook
Technical Editor: Nancy Mahoney
Copy Editor: Marcy Heffernan
Design Director: Stan Green
Production Manager: Regina Girard
Illustrator: Laurel Strand
Cover & Text Designer: Adrienne Smitke
Photographer: Brent Kane

Contents

Introduction

Twenty-five years ago when I learned to quilt, I was taught about "sandwich piecing." It's a simple concept where two strips are sewn together along both long edges. Triangles are then cut from the strip set. The result is pairs of triangles already sewn together along one edge.

Various types of triangles could be cut from the strip set, but in *Twin Peaks*, I only cut half-square triangles. The pairs of triangles are sewn together along their short sides unlike the usual half-square-triangle unit, in which you sew along the long side of the triangle. Using this method is quicker than handling little individually cut triangles—a bonus in any quilter's busy life.

Twin Peaks unit

Half-square triangle unit

I never understood why this method was called sandwich piecing as there was no "meat" or middle layer such as the batting in a quilt sandwich. With so much to learn and so many techniques to try, I didn't make a quilt with the technique at the time. Years later I saw a picture of a quilt I wanted to make and figured out how to make it using sandwich piecing. So, I made the quilt and changed the name of the technique to Twin Peaks.

Occasionally I found myself exploring the Twin Peaks technique to see what other designs I could come up with. Since then, I've published a few patterns using the technique, including two quilts in my book, *Save the Scraps* (Martingale & Company, 2005). I found I couldn't stop playing with Twin Peaks.

This book is not a basic quiltmaking manual, rather it is intended to provide one more method for the modern piecer to experience. Here you'll discover what I learned while experimenting with the technique as well as basic quilt finishing instructions. In between you'll find patterns for 13 quilts using Twin Peaks.

I hope you enjoy my quilts and use Twin Peaks to make your own beautiful quilts.

Basic Twin Peaks Construction

The Twin Peak technique is as easy as it looks. This section will tell you everything you need to know to master this method.

Basic Rotary Cutting

The projects in this book use basic rotary-cutting techniques that are familiar to most quilters. If you need more information, there are many good reference books available. Rotary-cutting tools include a rotary cutter, a cutting mat, and a 24" acrylic straight-edged ruler for cutting strips.

1. Cut strips the width listed in the cutting instructions for your project. Place two strips right sides together and raw edges aligned. Sew the strips together along both long edges to form a tube, called a strip set. Press the strips to set the seams.

Cut strips and sew into tubes.

2. Cut the strip set into squares the same dimension as the strip width. For example, if the strips are 2⅞" wide, you'll cut 2⅞" squares. Cut each square once diagonally immediately after cutting it from the strip. This will save you the time it takes to stack the squares out of the way and then reposition them again later to make the diagonal cut. Another reason to make the diagonal cuts right away is to prevent you from

accidentally changing the orientation of the squares. This is important in some designs, as you will see in "Diagonal Dilemma" at right. As you cut the triangles, stack them so they are all oriented the same way. This will make it easier to press the seam allowance of each unit in the same direction.

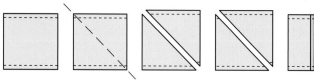

Cut squares, then cut once diagonally through the corners of each square.

3. Generally you'll press the seam allowance in all of the Twin Peaks units in the same direction. Carefully separate the two triangles where they are held together by two or three stitches. Hold the point with one hand while gently pressing with the other to prevent the bias edges from stretching. If you don't use steam, there is less danger of burning your finger as you hold the point.

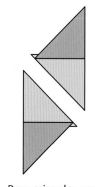

Press triangles open as indicated in the pattern.

The Twin Peaks units really are pretty easy to make, but it is helpful to have a thorough understanding before proceeding with one of the projects. So here are the specifics:

Diagonal Dilemma

Notice that when the squares are all cut diagonally in the same direction, all of the Twin Peaks units will look alike. For pinwheel designs like "Spin Off" on page 58, you'll only use identical Twin Peaks units.

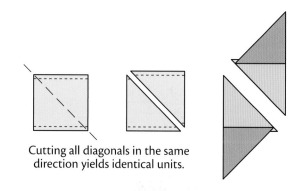

Cutting all diagonals in the same direction yields identical units.

The squares could be cut diagonally in both directions by alternating the diagonal cut from square to square. This will yield mirror-image units that are used in other designs such as "Farmer's Favorite" on page 44.

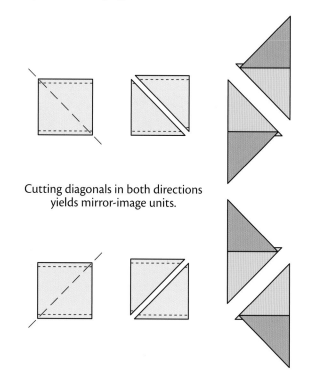

Cutting diagonals in both directions yields mirror-image units.

It's important to be aware that changing the placement of the fabric or the direction of stitching lines is the same as cutting the diagonal in the opposite direction. Study the illustration below to see what I mean.

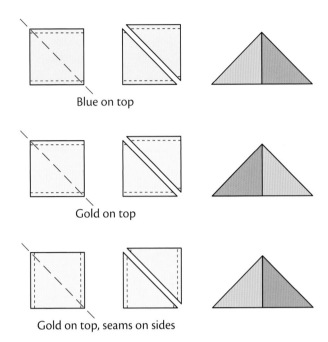

Blue on top

Gold on top

Gold on top, seams on sides

The direction to cut the diagonal will depend on the desired results. The project instructions clearly state how to make the diagonal cuts for the quilt you are making. In the quilts that use medium and dark prints together for a scrappy effect, it's not important which fabric is on top or which direction the diagonal is cut, but read on.

Scrap Combinations

Make sure you choose fabrics for scrappy Twin Peaks units that have some contrast but still blend together so that the two triangles read as one mulitcolor triangle. To achieve the desired results, be sure there is a high contrast between the medium or dark color prints and the lighter background print. Also avoid prints with both light and dark areas or the result will look busy or spotty.

Often when I make a scrap quilt, I cut strips from my collection of fat quarters to get the range of colors I want. The cutting instructions indicate 20"-long strips are required, assuming you may also cut your strips from assorted fat quarters. Though any strip length could be used, these shorter strips will add a greater variety of prints and more interest to the quilt.

To handle these, first sort the strips into two piles of similar fabrics. You could separate mediums from darks, or warm colors from cool colors, or reds from blues. The goal is to have some contrast between the two triangles in the unit. Use the strips from one pile as the top strip and the other pile as the bottom strip as you sew them together into strip sets.

To increase the number of print combinations further, stagger the strips as you sew them together to make one long strip set. There's no need to sew the short ends of the strips together before making the strip. Start by folding one strip in half to find the middle. Then place a second strip on top of the first strip, right sides together, aligning the beginning of the second strip with the middle of the first strip. Sew the strips together. When you reach the end of a strip, simply butt another up to it, whether it is on the top or bottom. Just make sure you position the fabric right sides together. When you have sewn all the strips together, sew along the opposite edge completing the tube. Press the strips to smooth the seams. And yes, the strip set could be 25 feet long.

If you staggered your strips, you will need to flip the strip set over after cutting a few squares in order to see the start of the next fabric. Trim off and discard selvages as you go and any section where the strips abut. Alternatively, you could cut the long strip set apart at the start of each different fabric, making segments of each combination of prints before you cut the squares. Cut the squares, and then make the diagonal cut, alternating the direction of each diagonal cut to really mix up the placement of the colors. This way the triangles will look more randomly sewn and not strip pieced.

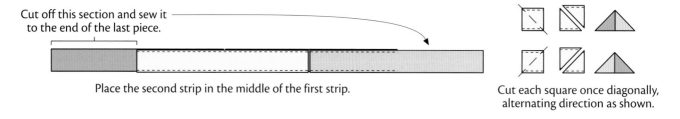

Cut off this section and sew it to the end of the last piece.

Place the second strip in the middle of the first strip.

Cut each square once diagonally, alternating direction as shown.

Even More Details

The math we use to determine the strip width for the Twin Peaks units is the same formula we use for rotary cutting template-free half-square triangles. If the finished size of the triangle is measured on the *short* side of the triangle, and it is on the straight of grain, then the triangle is a half-square triangle. Strips are cut ⅞" larger than the finished size of the triangle. (For example, cut strips 2⅞" wide for a 2" finished triangle.) Feel free to scale the designs up or down to suit your needs.

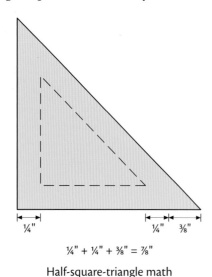

$$\frac{1}{4}" + \frac{1}{4}" + \frac{3}{8}" = \frac{7}{8}"$$

Half-square-triangle math

If you like to plan your own quilts, be careful not to mistake pairs of quarter-square triangles for Twin Peaks units. If the finished size of the triangle is measured on the *long* side of the triangle and it is on the straight of grain, then the triangle is

a quarter-square triangle and the Twin Peaks method should not be used, so choose patterns accordingly.

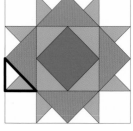

Twin Peaks unit   Quarter-square-triangle pair

Substituting Narrower Strips

Many avid quilters have their scraps cut and sorted into commonly used widths. You can use narrower strips from your scrap box, and then use an acrylic triangle-cutting ruler to cut triangles from the strips. Be sure to follow the manufacturer's instructions for using the ruler. The resulting triangles have one blunted tip; you'll simply need to use a seam ripper to pop one stitch in the seam at the blunted end of the triangles before pressing the triangles open.

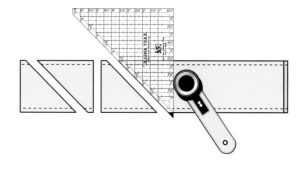

And finally, if you have a collection of the correct size half-square triangles in your stash, you're welcome to substitute them for the Twin Peaks units in any pattern in this book.

Trimming Points

I usually trim the extended seam allowance (often called "ears") at the triangle points after I sew pieces together, but sometimes trimming before sewing can make it easier to accurately align the pieces for stitching. I find trimming points particularly helpful when working with quarter-square triangles.

I use a template to trim these points at both angles because not all designs need to be trimmed at the same angle. There are rulers specifically made for trimming rotary cut triangles, or you could substitute any of the many commercially made acrylic templates that have a trimmed 45° angle. You can copy the pattern below onto template material, but mostly I included it here to show you what to look for at the store or in your box of quilting supplies.

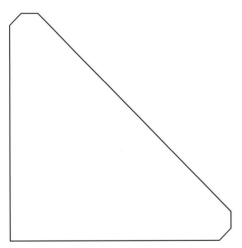

Point-trimming pattern for 45° triangles

After rotary cutting any size triangle, place the trimming template over the point to be trimmed, aligning the raw edges perfectly with the template. Trim away the excess at the tip. Rotate the template to trim the other point. Do this right after making the diagonal cuts, before the layers shift.

Here the triangle needs to be trimmed perpendicular to the long edge.

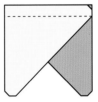

Here the triangles need to be trimmed perpendicular to the short edges.

My Best Tip

The best tip I can give for ensuring neat patchwork with crisp points and perfectly matched seam intersections is to sew an accurate quilters' ¼" seam allowance. If you have trouble getting the pieces to fit together easily and accurately, be sure to test your presser foot following the guidelines below.

Cut three pieces of fabric, each 1½" x 5", and using a ¼"-wide seam allowance, sew them together along their long edges as shown. Press and measure the width of the three-strip unit. It should now be exactly 3½" wide, with the center strip measuring 1" wide. If it does not, adjust the seam allowance by taking a slightly wider or narrower seam allowance until you find the correct width. When the correct seam allowance is used, you will see that it is actually a scant ¼", or what I call a quilter's ¼". It is necessary to use this seam allowance consistently in order to obtain the correct finished dimensions of any template-free, rotary-cut project.

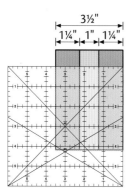

On some machines, finding and following a quilter's ¼" seam allowance is as simple as lining up your fabric with a quilting presser foot or moving the needle to the correct position. Additionally, you can mark the throat plate of your machine with several layers of masking tape once you've found where to properly position your fabric. Feeding the fabric against the edge of the layered tape will relieve eyestrain and help you sew more quickly. Repeat the test above with the tape in place to be certain it is positioned accurately. This is important because some machines feed the fabric at an angle, and the seam allowance width can be affected.

Pressing

The most important point when it comes to pressing is to handle the pieces gently to avoid stretching the bias edge. Remember it's the heat of the iron that sets the seam allowance in the direction you want it to go; do not use force to push the iron around and stretch the edges. Instead, gently glide the iron in the direction the threads run to help prevent stretched bias edges. Generally, press all the seam allowances in the Twin Peaks units in the same direction. In a few projects this would cause the seam allowances in later units to overlap and be bulky, so I flip those seam allowances and then re-press them to flatten the seam allowance in the opposite direction.

Throughout the projects I have given pressing suggestions indicated by arrows in the illustrations. These directions will result in seam allowances that will oppose one another and will make matching the seams practically effortless. In a few instances, twisted seams can't be avoided. There's no reason to worry; you'll stop stressing out. Or you can always press the seam allowances open.

In some blocks, you can create opposing seam allowances and reduce the bulk where four seams come together. After the seam is sewn, but before pressing, use a seam ripper to remove one or two stitches from the seam allowance. Then gently reposition the seam allowance as shown to evenly distribute the fabric. Press the seam allowances in a pinwheel fashion and they will be opposed when sewing them to the next unit.

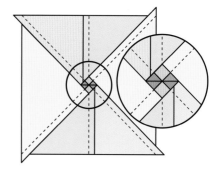

Borders

Once your blocks are sewn together, it's time to add the borders. Don't be tempted to simply apply the border strips without measuring. If you skip this important step, you could easily make the border several inches too long on one side or the other of your quilt. If the borders on opposite sides of your quilt are different lengths, the quilt won't have square corners and won't lie flat. This extra fabric is not easily quilted out and can result in wavy or rippling borders.

Border strips are generally cut crosswise, selvage to selvage, and joined end to end where necessary for the required length. Backstitch these short seams and press the seam allowances open so they lie flat and are less conspicuous. Try to place the seams randomly around the quilt to make them even less noticeable.

I generally prefer to sew the top and bottom borders to the quilt first, and then sew the side borders. However, for some of the quilts I stitched the sides first, and then added the top and bottom borders so that I could cut fewer strips.

Follow these instructions when adding borders with blunted corners to your quilt:

1. Measure through the center of the quilt and along the two parallel edges to find the average width. I measure using the actual border strip rather than a ruler or tape measure. I mark the three lengths with pins and compare them. Then I cut two border strips to the average width.

Mark the width with pins.

2. Fold the two border strips in half and mark their centers with pins.
3. Fold the quilt in half in both directions and mark the center of each edge with a pin.
4. Matching the centers, pin and sew the borders to top and bottom of the quilt top. (I sew with the wrong side of the quilt facing me to make sure all the seam allowances fall in the intended direction.)
5. Repeat the process for the two remaining borders, measuring through the borders you just added.

Mark the length with pins.

Window Shopping

Pieced and quilted by Gayle Bong

Squares in a variety of medium and dark prints edge this quilt for an effective border that makes the blocks appear as though they are set on point and share corners.

Materials

Yardage is based on 42"-wide fabric.

3⅞ yards *total* of 20 assorted medium and dark prints for blocks, border, and binding

2⅜ yards of cream fabric for background

4 yards of fabric for backing*

66" x 78" piece of batting

See page 75 for backing options.

Cutting

Please read all the directions before starting.

From the assorted medium and dark prints, cut a total of:

28 strips, 2⅞" x 20"

7 binding strips, 2¼" x 42"

40 squares, 6½" x 6½"

40 squares, 4⅞" x 4⅞"; cut once diagonally to make 80 half-square triangles (2 squares *each* from 20 prints)

From the cream background fabric, cut:

6 strips, 5¼" x 42"; crosscut into 40 squares, 5¼" x 5¼". Cut twice diagonally to yield 160 quarter-square triangles.

5 strips, 4⅞" x 42"; crosscut into 40 squares, 4⅞" x 4⅞". Cut once diagonally to yield 80 half-square triangles.

3 strips, 4½" x 42"; crosscut into 20 squares, 4½" x 4½"

3 strips, 2½" x 42"; crosscut into 36 squares, 2½" x 2½"

Making the Star Blocks

After sewing each seam, press the seam allowances in the direction indicated by the arrows.

1. Place the 2⅞"-wide medium or dark strips right sides together with the *beginning* ends staggered about 10". Sew the strips together along *both* long edges to make a strip set. For detailed instructions see "Scrap Combinations" on page 13. Cut 80 squares, 2⅞" each, trimming and discarding any section that spans a seam. Cut each square once diagonally, alternating the direction of each diagonal cut as shown. Make 160 Twin Peaks units.

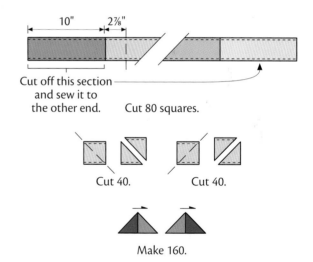

Cut off this section and sew it to the other end.   Cut 80 squares.

Cut 40.   Cut 40.

Make 160.

2. Sew a 5¼" cream triangle to each Twin Peaks unit as shown. Make 160 units. Sew two of these units together to make a star-point unit. Press the seam allowances in a pinwheel fashion so that they will oppose when sewing the star-point units to other units to make the block. Refer to "Pressing" on page 16 for more details. Make 80 star-point units.

Make 80.

3. Sew a 4⅞" cream triangle and a 4⅞" medium or dark triangle together; press. Make 80 half-square-triangle units.

Make 80.

4. To make a block, arrange four star-point units from step 2, four matching half-square-triangle units from step 3, and a 4½" cream square as shown. Sew the pieces into rows, and then sew the rows together. Make 20 blocks.

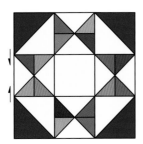

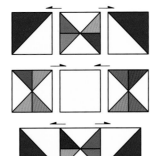

Make 20.

Quilt Assembly and Borders

1. Arrange the blocks as shown in the quilt assembly diagram on page 21. When you are happy with the color arrangement, sew the blocks into rows. Sew the rows together.

2. Set aside four medium or dark squares for the corners of the outer border. Draw a diagonal line from corner to corner on the wrong side of each 2½" cream square. Position a marked square on one corner of each remaining medium or dark square, right sides together and raw edges aligned. Sew along the marked line. Check your accuracy before trimming the seam allowance to ¼". (Wait to press the seam allowances until you've arranged the blocks as described in step 3.) Make 36 border units.

Make 36.

Folded Corners without Marking

Instead of drawing a diagonal line on the cream squares, you can mark your machine bed with a line coming straight toward you from the needle. (I use a 6" piece of masking tape.) When you're stitching, one corner will line up with the needle and the other corner will point at the line. As you sew, make sure that the corner exactly follows the line toward the needle.

3. Arrange the border units around the edge of the quilt as shown in the quilt assembly diagram. When you are happy with the color arrangement, sew the units into rows. Wait to press the rows until they are sewn to the quilt top so you can direct the seam allowances to oppose the seam allowances of the Star blocks. Sew the side borders to the quilt; then add the top and bottom borders.

Side border.
Make 2.

Top/bottom border.
Make 2.

Quilt assembly

4. Sew a line of stay stitching around the perimeter of the quilt top ³⁄₁₆" from the edge. This will prevent the seams in the pieced border from coming loose around the outer edge.

Finishing the Quilt

For detailed instructions on the following techniques, refer to "Finishing Techniques" on page 75.

1. Mark the quilting lines, if desired. Layer the quilt top with batting and backing; baste.
2. Hand or machine quilt. Follow the quilting suggestion shown below or use your own design.

Quilting diagram

3. Prepare the 2¼"-wide binding strips and sew the binding to the quilt.
4. Add a hanging sleeve if desired. Sign and date your quilt.

Chip off the Old Block

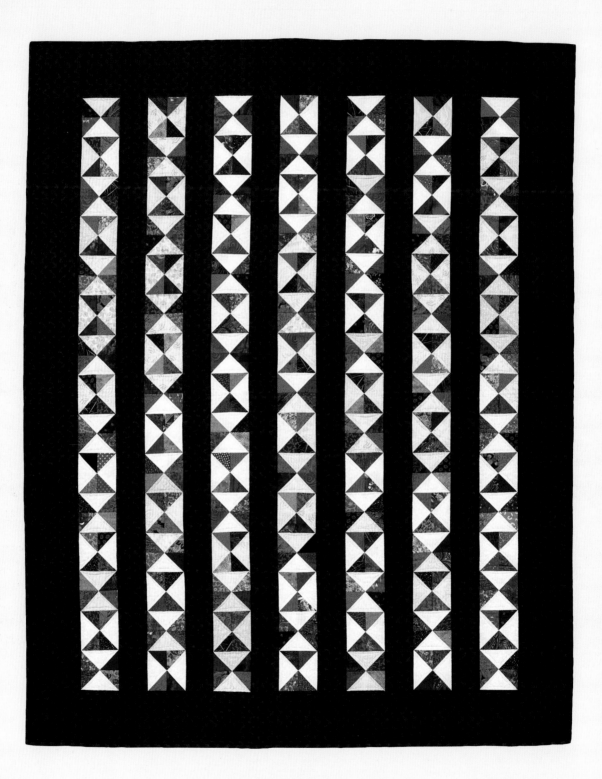

Pieced and quilted by Gayle Bong

This strip-set quilt offers a great change of pace. To enlarge it, consider starting with larger Twin Peaks units.

Materials

Yardage is based on 42"-wide fabric.

3¼ yards of navy blue fabric for sashing strips, border, and binding

1⅝ yards *total* of assorted medium and dark prints for blocks

1⅜ yards *total* of assorted cream prints for background

3⅞ yards of fabric for backing*

63" x 77" piece of batting

See page 75 for backing options.

Cutting

Please read all the directions before starting.

From the assorted medium and dark prints, cut:
36 strips, 2⅞" x 20"

From the assorted cream prints, cut:
8 strips, 5¼" x 42"; crosscut into 53 squares, 5¼" x 5¼". Cut twice diagonally to yield 212 quarter-square triangles. (You'll have 2 extra triangles.)

From the navy blue fabric, cut:
3 border strips, 6" x 42"
7 binding strips, 2¼" x 42"

From the *lengthwise* grain of the remaining navy blue fabric, cut:
2 border strips, 6" x 74"
6 strips, 3½" x 62"

Making the Blocks

After sewing each seam, press the seam allowances in the direction indicated by the arrows.

1. Place the 2⅞"-wide medium or dark strips right sides together with the *beginning* ends staggered about 10". Sew the strips together along *both* long edges to make a strip set. For detailed instructions see "Scrap Combinations" on page 13. Cut 105 squares, 2⅞" each, trimming and discarding any section that spans a seam. Cut each square once diagonally, alternating the direction of each diagonal cut as shown. Make 210 Twin Peaks units.

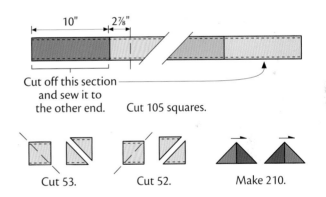

2. Sew a cream triangle to each Twin Peaks unit. Make 210 units. Sew two of these units together as shown to make a block. Press the seam allowances in a pinwheel fashion so that they will oppose when sewing the blocks together in the next step. Refer to "Pressing" on page 16 for more details. Make 105 blocks.

Make 105.

Quilt Assembly and Borders

1. Sew 15 blocks together to make a row, rotate every other block 90° as shown. Make three rows with a Twin Peaks unit at each end, and make four rows with a cream triangle at each end.

Make 3.

Make 4.

2. Measure the length of each of the seven rows. If they differ, calculate the average and consider this measurement the length. Trim the 3½"-wide sashing strips to fit that measurement. Mathematically, they should be 60½" long. Use pins to mark each row and each sashing strip at the center and quarter points. Match pins and ends. Take extra care to be sure the blocks align horizontally from row to row. Sew the rows and sashing strips together.

3. Referring to "Borders" on page 17, measure, cut, and sew the 6" x 42" navy blue strips to the top and bottom of the quilt top. Measure, cut, and sew the 6" x 74" strips to the sides of the quilt top for the outer border.

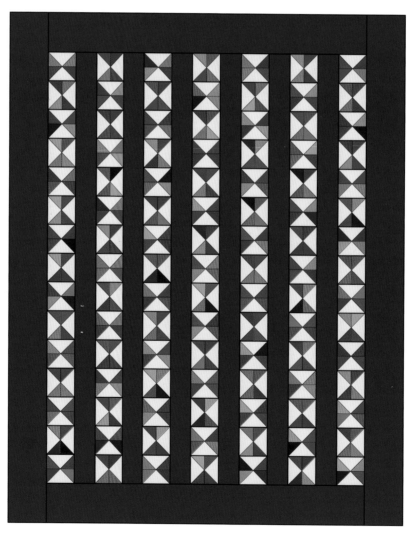

Quilt assembly

Finishing the Quilt

For detailed instructions on the following techniques, refer to "Finishing Techniques" on page 75.

1. Mark the quilting lines, if desired. Layer the quilt top with batting and backing; baste.
2. Hand or machine quilt. Follow the quilting suggestion shown at right or use your own design.
3. Prepare the 2¼"-wide binding strips and sew the binding to the quilt.
4. Add a hanging sleeve if desired. Sign and date your quilt.

Quilting diagram

Quilting with Joy

Pieced and quilted by Gayle Bong

Cheerful colors dance across this easy quilt. Make yours sparkle with your favorite colors and bring on the joy.

Materials

Yardage is based on 42"-wide fabric.

2⅝ yards of white fabric for block backgrounds and borders

2 yards *total* of assorted bright batiks for blocks and border

⅝ yard of fabric for binding

3⅝ yards of fabric for backing*

60" x 72" piece of batting

See page 75 for backing options.

Cutting

Please read all the directions before starting.

From the assorted bright batiks, cut:

28 strips, 3¼" x 20"

12 strips, 2½" x 20"

From the white fabric, cut:

7 strips, 6" x 42"; crosscut into 40 squares, 6" x 6". Cut twice diagonally to yield 160 quarter-square triangles.

11 border strips, 3½" x 42"

1 strip, 3¼" x 42"; crosscut into 8 squares, 3¼" x 3¼". Cut once diagonally to yield 16 half-square triangles.

From the binding fabric, cut:

7 strips, 2¼" x 42"

Making the Blocks

After sewing each seam, press the seam allowances in the direction indicated by the arrows.

1. Place the 3¼"-wide batik strips right sides together with the *beginning* ends staggered about 10". Sew the strips together along *both* long edges to make a strip set. For detailed instructions see "Scrap Combinations" on page 13. Cut 84 squares, 3¼" each, trimming and discarding any section that spans a seam. Cut each square once diagonally, alternating the direction of each diagonal cut as shown. Make 168 Twin Peaks units.

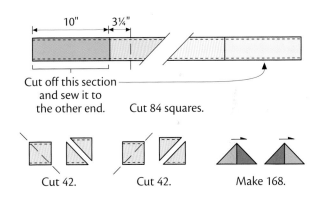

Cut off this section and sew it to the other end.

Cut 84 squares.

Cut 42. Cut 42. Make 168.

2. Sew each 6" white triangle to a Twin Peaks unit. Make 160 units. Sew two of these units together to make a block. Press the seam allowances in a pinwheel fashion so that they will oppose when sewing the blocks together in a later step. Refer to "Pressing" on page 16 for more details. Make 80 blocks.

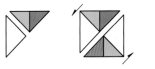

Make 80.

3. Sew a 3¼" white triangle to each end of a Twin Peaks unit as shown; press. Make eight half blocks.

Make 8.

Quilt Assembly and Borders

1. Sew 10 blocks together to make a row as shown. Add a half block to one end of each row; press. Make eight rows.

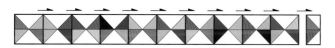

Make 8.

2. Refer to the quilt assembly diagram below to arrange the rows as shown. Rotate every other row so that alternate rows start with a half block. When you're happy with the color arrangement, sew the rows together.

3. Refer to "Borders" on page 17. Measure, cut, and sew five of the 3½"-wide white strips to the quilt top for the inner border.

4. Sewing diagonally across the corner, as shown, sew the 2½"-wide batik strips together end to end to make one long strip. Trim the seam allowance to ¼"; press the seam allowances open. Refer to "Borders" to measure, cut, and sew the batik strips to the quilt top for the middle border.

5. Using the remaining 3½"-wide strips, repeat step 3 to sew the outer border to the quilt top.

Quilt assembly

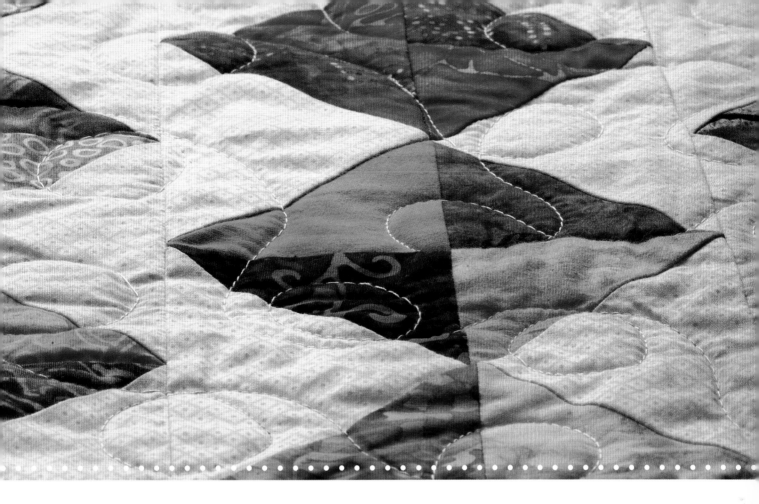

Finishing the Quilt

For detailed instructions on the following techniques, refer to "Finishing Techniques" on page 75.

1. Mark the quilting lines, if desired. Layer the quilt top with batting and backing; baste.
2. I quilted a meandering design my friend Joy uses on her quilts. It's fun and has a nice rhythm. Follow her design or use your own to hand or machine quilt.
3. Prepare the 2¼"-wide binding strips and sew the binding to the quilt.
4. Add a hanging sleeve if desired. Sign and date your quilt.

Quilting diagram

Queen for a Day

Pieced and quilted by Gayle Bong

This elegant quilt uses a variation of the old-fashioned Ohio Star block paired with Hourglass blocks. Using the same size Twin Peaks in the blocks and pieced border makes the border a natural fit and adds the crowning touch.

Materials

Yardage is based on 42"-wide fabric.

2½ yards of cream leaf print for Star blocks, setting triangles, and border

1⅓ yards *total* of assorted medium and dark prints for Star blocks and pieced border

1 yard of light cream background fabric for Hourglass blocks and pieced border

⅞ yard of dark leaf print for Hourglass blocks and setting triangles

⅝ yard of fabric for binding

4 yards of fabric for backing*

70" x 70" piece of batting

See page 75 for backing options.

Cutting

Please read all the directions before starting.

From the assorted medium and dark prints, cut:

26 strips, 2⅞" x 20"

5 dark squares, 4½" x 4½"

From the cream leaf print, cut:

7 border strips, 4½" x 42"

2 squares, 13¼" x 13¼"; cut twice diagonally to yield 8 quarter-square triangles

2 squares, 12⅞" x 12⅞"; cut once diagonally to yield 4 half-square triangles

10 squares, 5¼" x 5¼"; cut twice diagonally to yield 40 quarter-square triangles

20 squares, 4½" x 4½"

From the light cream background fabric, cut:

5 strips, 3⅜" x 42"; crosscut into 52 squares, 3⅜" x 3⅜"

2 squares, 13¼" x 13¼"; cut twice diagonally to yield 8 quarter-square triangles

From the dark leaf print, cut:

2 strips, 13¼" x 42"; crosscut into 5 squares, 13¼" x 13¼". Cut twice diagonally to yield 20 quarter-square triangles.

From the binding fabric, cut:

7 strips, 2¼" x 42"

Making the Star Blocks

After sewing each seam, press the seam allowances in the direction indicated by the arrows.

1. Place the 2⅞"-wide medium or dark strips right sides together with the *beginning* ends staggered about 10". Sew the strips together along *both* long edges to make a strip set. For detailed instructions see "Scrap Combinations" on page 13. Cut 72 squares, 2⅞" each, trimming and discarding any section that spans a seam. Cut each square once diagonally, alternating the direction of each diagonal cut as shown. Make 144 Twin Peaks units.

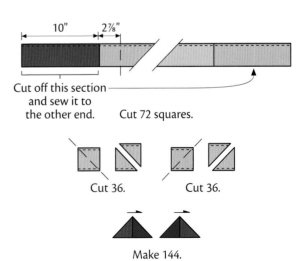

2. Sew each 5¼" cream leaf triangle to a Twin Peaks unit. Sew two of these units together as shown to make a star-point unit. Press the seam allowances in a pinwheel fashion so that they will oppose when sewing the star-point units to other units in the next step. Refer to "Pressing" on page 16 for more details. Make 20 units. (You'll use the remaining Twin Peaks units in "Making the Pieced Borders.")

Make 20.

3. To make a block, lay out four star-point units from step 2, four 4½" cream leaf squares, and one 4½" dark square as shown. Sew the pieces together into rows; join the rows to complete a block. Make five blocks.

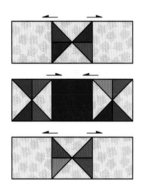 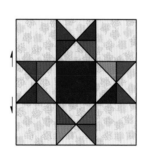

Make 5.

Making the Hourglass Blocks

Sew two light cream triangles and two dark leaf triangles together as shown to make a block; press. Make four Hourglass blocks.

Make 4.

Making the Pieced Borders

1. Sew a Twin Peaks unit to adjacent sides of a light cream square. Make 12 end units.

Make 12.

2. Sew two end units together to make a corner unit. Make four corner units.

Make 4.

3. Sew a Twin Peaks unit to opposite sides of each remaining light cream square to make 40 border units.

Make 40.

4. Sew 10 border units from step 3 and one end unit from step 1 together as shown; press. Make four border strips.

Make 4.

Quilt Assembly and Borders

1. Arrange the blocks in three rows, of three blocks each, alternating the Star blocks and Hourglass blocks in each row and from row to row. Sew the blocks in each row together; press. Sew the rows together; press.

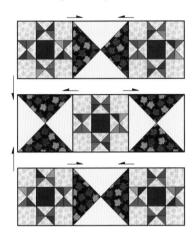

2. Refer to "Trimming Points" on page 15 to trim the corners of the triangles and sew three dark leaf triangles and two 13¼" cream leaf triangles together as shown to make a setting-triangle unit. Make four units. Sew these to the quilt top as shown in the quilt assembly diagram at right.

Make 4.

3. Fold the 12⅞" cream leaf triangles in half and lightly crease to mark the center of the long side. Sew the triangles to the quilt top, matching the center crease with the corner of a Star block as shown; press.

4. Sew a pieced border strip to each side of the quilt top, matching centers and extending the point of a border triangle ⅜" beyond the edge of the quilt top.

5. Add the corner units to complete the pieced border.

Match crease to corner of block.

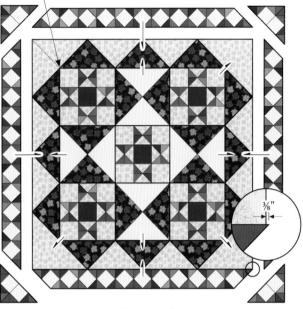

Quilt assembly

6. Refer to "Borders" on page 17 to measure, cut, and sew the 4½"-wide cream leaf strips to the quilt top for the outer border.

Finishing the Quilt

For detailed instructions on the following techniques, refer to "Finishing Techniques" on page 75.

1. Mark the quilting lines, if desired. Layer the quilt top with batting and backing; baste.
2. Hand or machine quilt. Follow the quilting suggestion shown at right or use your own design.
3. Prepare the 2¼"-wide binding strips and sew the binding to the quilt.
4. Add a hanging sleeve if desired. Sign and date your quilt.

Quilting diagram

Faded Sunflowers

Pieced and quilted by Gayle Bong

Rearranging the values, limiting the use of color, and setting on the diagonal disguise the fact that the blocks in this quilt are constructed the same way as the blocks in "Window Shopping" on page 18.

Materials

Yardage is based on 42"-wide fabric.

3⅜ yards of green fabric for blocks, border, and binding

2¼ yards of cream fabric for background

⅞ yard of rust fabric for blocks

⅝ yard of peach fabric for blocks

5 yards of fabric for backing*

65" x 82" piece of batting

See page 75 for backing options.

Cutting

Please read all the directions before starting.

From the cream background fabric, cut:

6 strips, 4⅞" x 42"; crosscut *1 of the strips* into 7 squares, 4⅞" x 4⅞". Cut once diagonally to yield 14 half-square triangles.

6 inner-border strips, 3" x 42"

7 strips, 2⅞" x 42"

From the green fabric, cut:

4 strips, 5¼" x 42"; crosscut into 23 squares, 5¼" x 5¼". Cut twice diagonally to yield 92 quarter-square triangles.

7 outer-border strips, 5" x 42"

3 strips, 4½" x 42"; crosscut into 18 squares, 4½" x 4½"

7 strips, 2⅞" x 42"

7 binding strips, 2¼" x 42"

2 squares, 3¾" x 3¾"; cut once diagonally to yield 4 half-square triangles

From the peach fabric, cut:

3 strips, 5¼" x 42"; crosscut into 18 squares, 5¼" x 5¼". Cut twice diagonally to yield 72 quarter-square triangles.

From the rust fabric, cut:

5 strips, 4⅞" x 42"

Making the Blocks

After sewing each seam, press the seam allowances in the direction indicated by the arrows.

1. Place a 2⅞"-wide green strip on top of a 2⅞"-wide cream strip, right sides together. Sew the strips together along *both* long edges. Make seven strip sets. For detailed instructions see "Basic Twin Peaks Construction" on page 11. With the green strip on top, cut 82 squares, 2⅞" each, and then cut each square once diagonally, alternating the direction of each diagonal cut as shown. Make 164 Twin Peaks units (82 of each).

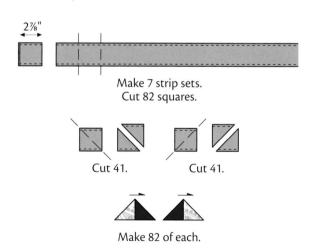

2⅞"

Make 7 strip sets.
Cut 82 squares.

Cut 41.   Cut 41.

Make 82 of each.

2. Sew a 5¼" green triangle to the cream triangle of a Twin Peaks unit as shown. Make 72 green-triangle units. Sew a 5¼" peach triangle to the green triangle of a Twin Peaks unit as shown. Make 72 peach-triangle units.

Make 72.   Make 72.

3. Sew a green-triangle unit and a peach-triangle unit together as shown. Press the seam allowances in a pinwheel fashion so that they will oppose when sewing the units together in a later step. Refer to "Pressing" on page 16 for more details. Make 72 units.

Make 72.

4. Place a 4⅞" cream strip on top of a 4⅞" rust strip, right sides together and raw edges aligned; press the strips together. Repeat with the other four pairs of strips. Crosscut the strips into 34 pairs of squares, 4⅞" each. Without disturbing the squares, cut each pair of cream/rust squares once diagonally to make pairs of half-square triangles that are ready to sew. Sew the triangle pairs together to make 68 half-square-triangle units.

Make 68.

5. Use the green squares, 3¾" green triangles, cream triangles, and the units from steps 3 and 4 to arrange the blocks as shown. Join the pieces into rows, and then sew the rows together. Make eight blocks with rust triangles in four corners. Make six side blocks with rust triangles in three corners and a cream triangle

in one corner. Make four corner blocks with rust triangles in two corners, cream triangles in two corners, and a green triangle on top as shown.

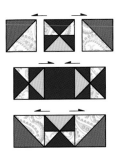 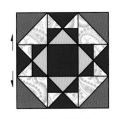

Make 8 blocks.

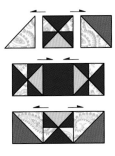 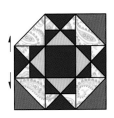

Make 6 side blocks.

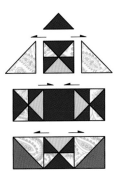 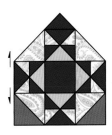

Make 4 corner blocks.

6. Sew a 5¼" green triangle to the cream triangle of each remaining Twin Peaks unit as shown. Make 10 of each unit (20 total).

Make 10 of each.

7. Sew two units from step 6 to each remaining half-square-triangle unit from step 4 as shown to make a partial block. Make 10 partial blocks.

Make 10
partial blocks.

Quilt Assembly and Borders

1. Arrange the blocks and partial blocks as shown at right. Sew the blocks into diagonal rows, and then sew the rows together.

2. Refer to "Borders" on page 17 to measure, cut, and sew the 3"-wide cream inner-border strips and then the 5"-wide green outer-border strips to the quilt top.

Quilt assembly

Finishing the Quilt

For detailed instructions on the following techniques, refer to "Finishing Techniques" on page 75.

1. Mark the quilting lines, if desired. Layer the quilt top with batting and backing; baste.
2. Hand or machine quilt. Follow the quilting suggestion shown at right or use your own design.
3. Prepare the 2¼"-wide binding strips and sew the binding to the quilt.
4. Add a hanging sleeve if desired. Sign and date your quilt.

Quilting diagram

Rust Spots

Pieced by Gayle Bong and quilted by Judy Johnson

The easy-to-piece border was the starting point for this stunning quilt. The blocks are constructed in diagonal rows to accommodate the Twin Peaks technique.

Materials

Yardage is based on 42"-wide fabric.

3 yards *total* of assorted medium and dark prints for blocks

2⅜ yards of cream fabric for background

2 yards of rust fabric for border and binding

5 yards of fabric for backing*

66" x 82" piece of batting

See page 75 for backing options.

Cutting

Please read all the directions before starting.

From the assorted medium and dark prints, cut:

44 strips, 2⅞" x 20"

34 squares, 4⅞" x 4⅞"; cut once diagonally to yield 68 half-square triangles

From the cream background fabric, cut:

3 strips, 6⅛" x 42"; crosscut into 17 squares, 6⅛" x 6⅛"

7 strips, 5¼" x 42"; crosscut into 44 squares, 5¼" x 5¼". Cut twice diagonally to yield 176 quarter-square triangles.

2 strips, 3⅜" x 42"; crosscut into 18 squares, 3⅜" x 3⅜"

3 strips, 2⅞" x 42"; crosscut into 36 squares, 2⅞" x 2⅞". Cut once diagonally to yield 72 half-square triangles.

2 squares, 4⅞" x 4⅞"; cut once diagonally to make 4 half-square triangles

From the rust fabric, cut:

7 outer-border strips, 4½" x 42"

5 inner-border strips, 2½" x 42"

8 binding strips, 2¼" x 42"

Making Block A

After sewing each seam, press the seam allowances in the direction indicated by the arrows.

1. Place the medium or dark strips right sides together with the *beginning* ends staggered about 10". Sew the strips together along *both* long edges to make a strip set. For detailed instructions see "Scrap Combinations" on page 13. Cut 128 squares, 2⅞" each, trimming and discarding any section that spans a seam. Cut each square once diagonally, alternating the direction of each diagonal cut as shown. Make 256 Twin Peaks units.

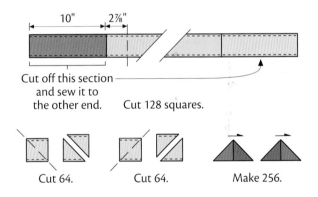

Cut off this section and sew it to the other end.   Cut 128 squares.

Cut 64.   Cut 64.   Make 256.

2. Sew the Twin Peaks units together in pairs to make 72 hourglass units. Press the seam allowances in a pinwheel fashion so that they will oppose when sewing the blocks together in the next step. Refer to "Pressing" on page 16 for more details. (You'll use the remaining Twin Peaks units in the pieced border.)

Make 72.

3. Sew four hourglass units from step 2, one 3⅜" cream square, four 5¼" cream triangles, and four 2⅞" cream triangles together in diagonal rows. Sew the rows together to make a block. Make 18 of block A.

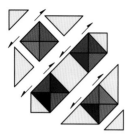

Make 18.

Making Block B

Fold each 6⅛" cream square in half vertically and horizontally, and lightly crease to mark the center of each side. Fold each 4⅞" medium or dark triangle in half, and lightly crease to mark the center of the long side. Sew triangles to opposite sides of each square, matching the center creases; press. Sew triangles to the remaining sides of the squares; press. Make 17 of block B.

Make 17.

Quilt Assembly and Borders

1. Arrange the blocks in seven rows of five blocks each, alternating A and B blocks as shown in the quilt assembly diagram on page 43. Play with the position of the blocks until you are happy with the color arrangement. Sew the blocks into rows, pressing the seam allowances toward the B blocks. Sew the rows together; press.

2. Refer to "Borders" on page 17 to measure, cut, and sew the 2½"-wide rust strips to the quilt top for the inner border.

3. Sew two Twin Peaks units together to make a triangle. Add a 4⅞" cream triangle to make a corner unit for the pieced middle border. Make four corner units.

Make 4.

4. Sew a 5¼" cream triangle to a Twin Peaks unit as shown. Make 104 units. Sew two of these units together to make a border unit. Press the seam allowances in a pinwheel fashion so that they will oppose when sewing the border units together in the next step. Refer to "Pressing" on page 16 for details. Make 52 border units.

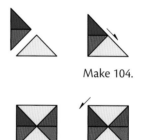

Make 104.

Make 52.

5. Sew 15 border units together to make a side-border strip. Make two, and sew them to the sides of the quilt top.

Side border.
Make 2.

6. Sew 11 border units together for the top- and bottom-border strips. Sew a corner unit from step 3 to both ends of each border strip as

shown. Sew the strips to the top and bottom of the quilt top as shown in the quilt assembly diagram.

Top/bottom border.
Make 2.

7. Refer to "Borders" to measure, cut, and sew the 4½"-wide rust strips to the quilt top for the outer border.

Finishing the Quilt

For detailed instructions on the following techniques, refer to "Finishing Techniques" on page 75.

1. Mark the quilting lines, if desired. Layer the quilt top with batting and backing; baste.
2. I used another quilt top for the backing, so I chose a meandering design that would work with either side. Another quilting suggestion is shown below, or use your own design to hand or machine quilt.

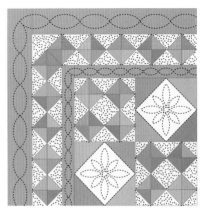

Quilting diagram

3. Prepare the 2¼"-wide binding strips and sew the binding to the quilt.
4. Add a hanging sleeve if desired. Sign and date your quilt.

Quilt assembly

Farmer's Favorite

Pieced by Gayle Bong and quilted by Judy Johnson

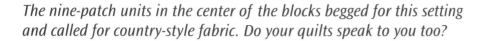

The nine-patch units in the center of the blocks begged for this setting and called for country-style fabric. Do your quilts speak to you too?

Materials

Yardage is based on 42"-wide fabric.

5⅞ yards *total* of 12–15 assorted cream prints for borders and background

2½ yards *total* of 12–15 assorted dark prints for blocks and sashing

¼ yard *each* of 12 assorted medium prints for blocks

3½ yards of brown fabric for borders and binding

8¼ yards of fabric for backing*

90" x 109" piece of batting

See page 75 for backing options.

Cutting

Please read all the directions before starting.

For the Blocks

For each of the 12 different blocks, you'll find it helpful to choose a set of three fabrics, a cream background, a medium print, and a dark print. As you cut and sew, keep the pieces together so that you have all the matching pieces you need for each block.

From *each* of 12 of the assorted cream prints, cut:

1 strip, 3" x 13" (12 total)

1 square, 5½" x 5½" (12 total); cut twice diagonally to yield 48 quarter-square triangles

2 squares, 5⅛" x 5⅛" (24 total); cut once diagonally to yield 48 half-square triangles

4 squares, 2½" x 2½" (48 total)

From *each* of 12 of the assorted dark prints, cut:

1 strip, 3" x 13" (12 total)

5 squares, 2½" x 2½" (60 total)

From *each* of the 12 assorted medium prints, cut:

2 squares, 5⅛" x 5⅛" (24 total); cut once diagonally to yield 48 half-square triangles

For the Sashing and Borders

From the remaining assorted dark prints, cut a *total* of:

31 rectangles, 2½" x 13¼"

100 squares, 2½" x 2½" (You'll need 20 sets of 5 matching squares.)

From the remaining assorted cream prints, cut a *total* of:

8 inner-border strips, 2½" x 42"*

26 strips, 2½" x 42"; crosscut into

- 62 rectangles, 2½" x 13¼"
- 80 squares, each 2½" x 2½" (You'll need 20 sets of 4 matching squares.)

4 squares, 4½" x 4½"

From the brown fabric, cut:

9 outer-border strips, 7½" x 42"

8 inner-border strips, 2½" x 42"

10 binding strips, 2¼" x 42"

I used a different cream print in the border on each side of the quilt. To make yours like mine, set aside four pairs of different print strips 2½" x 42" (8 total).

Making the Blocks

After sewing each seam, press the seam allowances in the direction indicated by the arrows. Each block is made using the pieces from one cream, one medium print, and one dark print.

1. To make each block, place a dark strip on top of a cream strip, right sides together, and sew the strips together along *both* long edges. For detailed instructions see "Basic Twin Peaks Construction" on page 11. Make 12 strip sets. Cut four squares, 3" each, from each strip set (48 total). Cut each square once diagonally, alternating the direction of the diagonal cut as shown. Make four and four reverse Twin Peaks units from each strip set (96 total).

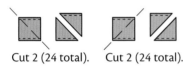

Make 12 strip sets.
Cut 4 squares from each.

Cut 2 (24 total).   Cut 2 (24 total).

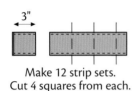

Make 48 of each.

2. Sew Twin Peaks units to adjacent sides of a medium print triangle as shown. Make four.

Make 4.

3. Sew a 5⅛" cream triangle to each unit from step 2. Make four.

Make 4.

4. Sew 5½" cream triangles to opposite sides of a unit from step 3 as shown. Make two.

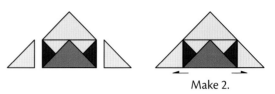

Make 2.

5. Make a nine-patch unit using four cream squares and five dark squares. Sew the squares into rows, and then sew the rows together.

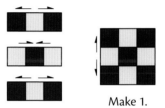

Make 1.

6. Sew a nine-patch unit and two units from step 3 together as shown. Then add the units from step 4 to complete a block.

Make 1.

7. Repeat steps 2–6 to make a total of 12 blocks using a different set of three fabrics for each block.

Making the Sashing and Cornerstones

1. Make a nine-patch unit using four matching 2½" cream squares and five matching dark squares. Sew the squares into rows, and then sew the rows together; press. Make 20 nine-patch units.

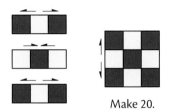

Make 20.

2. Sew each dark rectangle between two cream rectangles; press. Make 31 sashing units.

Make 31.

Quilt Assembly and Borders

1. Arrange and sew together four nine-patch units and three sashing units, alternating them as shown to make a sashing row; press. Make five rows.

Make 5.

2. Arrange and sew together four sashing units and three blocks, alternating them as shown to make a block row; press. Make four rows.

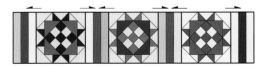

Make 4.

3. Sew the block rows and sashing rows together, alternating them as shown in the quilt assembly diagram below. Press the seam allowances toward the sashing rows.

4. Sew two matching 2½"-wide cream strips together end to end to make a long strip. Make four long cream strips. Repeat using the 2½"-wide brown strips to make four long brown strips. Sew a long cream strip and a long brown strip together along their long edges to make a border strip; press. For the side-border strips, measure the quilt through the center from top to bottom and cut two strips from the border strips to fit that measurement. For the top and bottom borders, measure the quilt top through the center from side to side and cut two strips from the remaining border strips to fit that measurement. Sew the side borders to the quilt top. Refer to "Borders" on page 17 for details as needed.

5. Sew a 4½" cream square to both ends of each short border strip and sew the border strips to the top and bottom of the quilt top.

6. Referring to "Borders," measure, cut, and sew the 7½"-wide brown strips to the quilt top for the outer border.

Quilt assembly

Finishing the Quilt

For detailed instructions on the following techniques, refer to "Finishing Techniques" on page 75.

1. Mark the quilting lines, if desired. Layer the quilt top with batting and backing; baste.
2. I selected a basic meandering quilt design for my long-arm quilter to follow. Refer to the quilting diagram for an alternate quilting suggestion, or use your own design to hand or machine quilt.
3. Prepare the 2¼"-wide binding strips and sew the binding to the quilt.
4. Add a hanging sleeve if desired. Sign and date your quilt.

Quilting diagram

Get Dizzy

Pieced by Gayle Bong and quilted by Judy Johnson

These playful pinwheels called for a cheery rainbow palette, perfect to delight your inner child as well as the inner child of someone you love.

Materials

Yardage is based on 42"- wide fabric.
2⅜ yards of white fabric 1 for background
¼ yard of white fabric 2 for background
⅜ yard *each* of pink, red, orange, yellow, green, medium blue, dark blue, and purple fabrics for blocks
⅝ yard of fabric for binding
3½ yards of fabric for backing*
58" x 70" piece of batting
See page 75 for backing options.

Cutting

Please read all the directions before starting.
From *each* of the pink, red, orange, yellow, green, medium blue, dark blue, and purple fabrics, cut:
1 strip, 4⅞" x 42" (8 total)
1 strip, 4⅞" x 11" (8 total)
8 squares, 2⅞" x 2⅞" (64 total); cut once diagonally to yield 128 half-square triangles. (You'll have 8 extra triangles.)

From the white background fabric 1, cut:
2 squares, 2⅞" x 2⅞"; crosscut once diagonally to yield 4 half-square triangles
5 strips, 11¼" x 42"; with strips open (unfolded) and *right side up*; crosscut 80 rectangles, 2½" x 11¼". Trim a 45° angle from each end of the rectangles as shown to make 80 parallelograms.

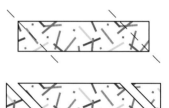

Cut 80.

6 strips, 2½" x 42"; crosscut into 18 rectangles, 2½" x 13¼". Trim a 45° angle from each end of the rectangles as shown to make 18 trapezoids.

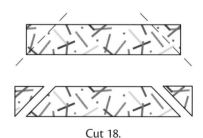

Cut 18.

From the white background fabric 2, cut:
2 strips, 3⅜" x 42"; crosscut into 20 squares, 3⅜" x 3⅜"

From the binding fabric, cut:
7 strips, 2¼" x 42"

Making the Blocks

After sewing each seam, press the seam allowances in the direction indicated by the arrows.

1. Place the 42"-long red strip and the 42"-long green strip, right sides together, and sew the strips together along *both* long edges as shown. Refer to "Basic Twin Peaks Construction" on page 11 for details. Repeat to sew the long medium blue and pink strips, the dark blue and yellow strips, and the purple and orange strips together. Pair and sew together the short strips in the same way as the long strips. Make one long strip set (four total) and one short strip set (four total) from each color combination. Making sure the cool colors (purple, medium blue, green, and dark blue) are on top, cut 10 squares from each color combination, 4⅞" each. Cut each square once diagonally as shown to make 20 Twin Peaks units (80 total).

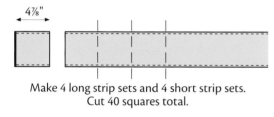

4⅞"

Make 4 long strip sets and 4 short strip sets.
Cut 40 squares total.

Cut all squares
at this angle.

Make 20 of each color combination.

2. Sew a white parallelogram to each Twin Peaks unit. Then add a 2⅞" triangle of any color print to the one end of the parallelogram as shown.

Make 80.

3. With right sides together, sew a red/green unit from step 2 to a white 3⅜" square leaving about 1½" open at the end of the square. Working in a clockwise direction around the white center square, sew the medium blue/pink unit, then the blue/yellow unit, and finally the purple/orange unit. After the last unit is added, sew the small open section of the center square seam closed to complete the block. Make 20 blocks. Be sure to sew all of the blocks in the same manner.

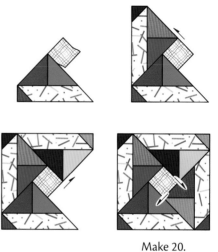

Make 20.

Quilt Assembly and Borders

1. Sew the blocks in five rows of four blocks each as shown in the quilt assembly diagram on page 52. Sew the rows together; press.

2. Sew a 2⅞" triangle of any color print to each end of the white trapezoids. Press the seam allowances in one direction. Make 18 units.

Make 18.

3. Sew a 2⅞" triangle of any color print to a white 2⅞" triangle; press. Make four half-square-triangle units.

Make 4.

4. Sew trapezoid units together to make four border strips as shown. Sew a half-square-triangle unit to both ends of each long border strip as shown.

Top/bottom border.
Make 2.

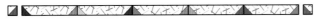

Side border.
Make 2.

5. Pin the border strip to the quilt, matching the seams and ends. Sew the short border strips to the quilt top; then add the long borders strips.

6. Sew a line of stay stitching ³⁄₁₆" from the edge of the quilt. This will prevent the seams in the pieced border from coming loose around the edge of the quilt.

Pressing Tip

Do not press the seam allowances between the units in the pieced border until you sew the border to the quilt. Then flip the seam allowances so they oppose the seam allowances between the blocks.

Quilt assembly

Finishing the Quilt

For detailed instructions on the following techniques, refer to "Finishing Techniques" on page 75.

1. Mark the quilting lines, if desired. Layer the quilt top with batting and backing; baste.
2. I chose a meandering quilt design of circles for my long-arm quilter to follow. Refer to the quilting diagram for an alternate quilting suggestion, or use your own design to hand or machine quilt.
3. Prepare the 2¼"-wide binding strips and sew the binding to the quilt.
4. Add a hanging sleeve if desired. Sign and date your quilt.

Quilting diagram

Show Your Spirit

Pieced and quilted by Gayle Bong

Quilts in patriotic colors are a great decoration for summer. I finished this as a tablecloth or summer quilt by leaving out the batting.

Materials

Yardage is based on 42"-wide fabric.
1½ yards of white fabric for background
1⅜ yards of blue fabric for blocks, border, and
  binding
1⅛ yard of tan fabric for blocks and inner border
⅜ yard of red fabric for blocks
3¼ yards of fabric for backing*
53" x 60" piece of batting
See page 75 for backing options.

Cutting

Please read all the directions before starting.
From the tan fabric, cut:
6 strips, 3½" x 42"
5 inner-border strips, 2¼" x 42"

From the blue fabric, cut:
3 strips, 3½" x 42"
5 outer-border strips, 3½ " x 42"
6 binding strips, 2¼" x 42"

From the red fabric, cut:
3 strips, 3½" x 42"

From the white background fabric, cut:
20 strips, 2¼" x 42"; crosscut into 120 rectangles,
  2¼" x 6"

Making the Blocks

After sewing each seam, press the seam allow-ances in the direction indicated by the arrows.

1. Place a 3½"-wide blue strip and a 3½"-wide tan strip right sides together, and sew them together along *both* long edges as shown. Make three strip sets. Refer to "Basic Twin Peaks Construction" on page 11 for details. Repeat to sew 3½"-wide red strips and 3½"-wide tan strips together. Make three strip sets. Cutting all of the strip sets with the blue or red print on top, cut 30 squares from each combination of fabrics, 3½" each. Cut each square once diagonally making sure to cut all diagonals in the same direction as shown. Make 60 blue/tan Twin Peaks units and 60 red/tan Twin Peaks units.

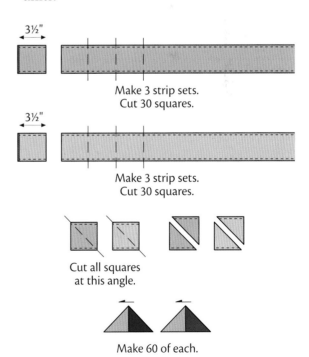

3½"

Make 3 strip sets.
Cut 30 squares.

3½"

Make 3 strip sets.
Cut 30 squares.

Cut all squares
at this angle.

Make 60 of each.

2. Sew a white rectangle to the tan side of each Twin Peaks unit as shown. Make 60 of each combination of fabrics.

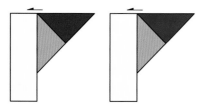

Make 60 of each.

3. Sew a blue unit to each red unit as shown to make a half block. Then sew two half blocks together. Press the center seam allowances in a pinwheel fashion so that they will oppose when sewing the blocks together. Refer to "Pressing" on page 16 for details. Make 30 blocks.

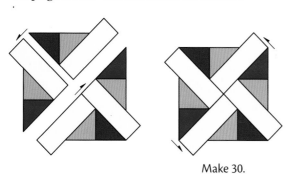

Make 30.

4. Square the blocks to 8", measuring 4" from the center point to trim each edge. Be sure the diagonal seams line up with the corners of the ruler. If possible, use an 8" (or larger) square ruler so you can measure and cut two edges without moving the ruler.

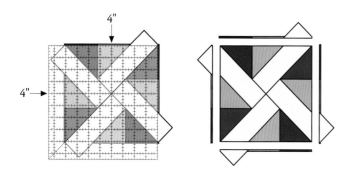

Quilt Assembly and Borders

1. Arrange the blocks in six rows of five blocks each, rotate every other block 90° to form red pinwheels and blue pinwheels. Sew the blocks into rows, and then sew the rows together; press.
2. Refer to "Borders" on page 17 to measure, cut, and sew the 2¼"-wide tan inner-border strips, and then the 3½"-wide blue outer-border strips to the quilt top.

Quilt assembly

Finishing the Quilt

For detailed instructions on the following techniques, refer to "Finishing Techniques" on page 75.

1. Mark the quilting lines, if desired. Layer the quilt top with batting and backing; baste.
2. Hand or machine quilt. Follow the quilting suggestion shown below or use your own design.

Quilting diagram

3. Prepare the 2¼"-wide binding strips and sew the binding to the quilt.
4. Add a hanging sleeve if desired. Sign and date your quilt.

Summer Quilts So Simple

My quilt is only slightly different from the instructions. Not only did I leave out the batting to make this a summer quilt, but I also omitted the binding. Instead of layering, quilting, and binding in that order, I finished the edge first, and then turned the quilt inside out.

Here is how I did it:

1. Using a ½"-wide seam allowance, sew the backing pieces together, leaving a 12" opening in the backing seam. Press the seam allowance to one side. On the wrong side, pin the opening closed. The opening in the back seam finishes more smoothly than a seam along the edge.
2. Secure the backing *right* side up on a flat surface using masking tape to keep it flat and taut, but not stretched.
3. Spread the quilt top *wrong* side up over the backing (right sides are together). Pin around the edges every 5".
4. Using a ¼" seam allowance, stitch around the entire perimeter of the quilt. Take one or two stitches diagonally at the corners for smooth turning. Trim close to the corners. Remove the pins.
5. Remove the pins from the opening in the backing, and turn the quilt right side out through the opening. Work the seam edges between the thumb and finger and direct the backing slightly to the back at the seam line; press.
6. Use a blind stitch to sew the opening in the backing closed.
7. Smooth out both layers and baste as you would for machine quilting. Stitch around the perimeter of the quilt, ¼" from the edge. Continue to stitch as desired to secure the layers together.

Spin Off

Pieced and quilted by Gayle Bong

I really enjoy experimenting with color placement in existing designs. Here's one variation of "Show Your Spirit" on page 54.

Materials

Yardage is based on 42"-wide fabric.

2⅜ yards of medium blue fabric for blocks and border

1¾ yards of cream fabric for inner border and background

1¼ yards of dark blue fabric for blocks and binding

1⅛ yards of medium green fabric for blocks

⅝ yard of dark green fabric for blocks

5 yards of fabric for backing*

66" x 81" piece of batting

See page 75 for backing options.

Cutting

Please read all the directions before starting.

From the dark green fabric, cut:
5 strips, 3½" x 42"

From the dark blue fabric, cut:
5 strips, 3½" x 42"
8 binding strips, 2¼" x 42"

From the cream fabric, cut:
10 strips, 3½" x 42"
6 inner-border strips, 3" x 42"

From the medium blue fabric, cut:
7 outer-border strips, 5½" x 42"
16 strips, 2¼" x 42"; crosscut into 96 rectangles, 2¼" x 6"

From the medium green fabric, cut:
16 strips, 2¼" x 42"; crosscut into 96 rectangles, 2¼" x 6"

Making the Blocks

After sewing each seam, press the seam allowances in the direction indicated by the arrows.

1. Place a 3½"-wide dark green strip and a 3½"-wide cream strip, right sides together, and sew the strips together along *both* long edges as shown. Make five strip sets. Refer to "Basic Twin Peaks Construction" on page 11 for details. Repeat to sew 3½"-wide dark blue strips and 3½"-wide cream strips together. Make five strip sets. Cutting all of the strip sets with the dark green or dark blue print on top, cut 48 squares from each combination of fabrics, 3½" each. Cut each square once diagonally, making sure to cut all diagonals in the same direction as shown. Make 96 dark green/cream Twin Peaks units and 96 dark blue/cream Twin Peaks units.

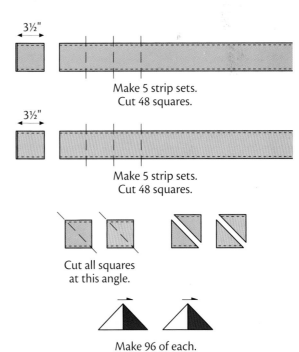

3½"

Make 5 strip sets.
Cut 48 squares.

3½"

Make 5 strip sets.
Cut 48 squares.

Cut all squares
at this angle.

Make 96 of each.

2. Sew a medium blue rectangle to the cream side of each dark green/cream Twin Peaks unit as shown. Make 96.

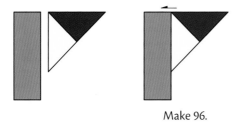

Make 96.

3. Sew a medium green rectangle to the cream side of each dark blue/cream Twin Peaks unit as shown. Make 96.

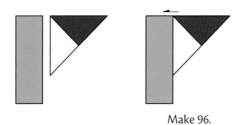

Make 96.

4. Sew the units from steps 2 and 3 together as shown to make a block. Press the center seam allowances in a pinwheel fashion so that they will oppose when sewing the blocks together. Refer to "Pressing" on page 16 for details. Make 48 blocks.

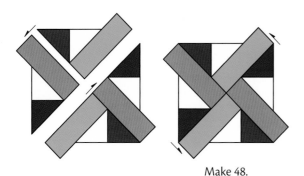

Make 48.

5. Square the blocks to 8", measuring 4" from the center point to trim each edge. Be sure the diagonal seams line up with the corners of the ruler. If possible, use an 8" (or larger) square

ruler so you can measure and cut two edges without moving the ruler.

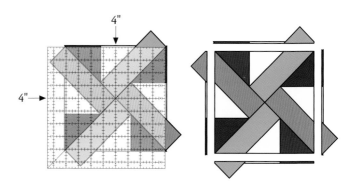

Quilt Assembly and Borders

1. Arrange the blocks in eight rows of six blocks each, rotate every other block 90° to form green pinwheels and blue pinwheels. Sew the blocks into rows, and then sew the rows together; press.
2. Refer to "Borders" on page 17 to measure, cut, and sew the 3"-wide cream inner-border strips and then the 5½"-wide medium blue outer-border strips to the quilt top.

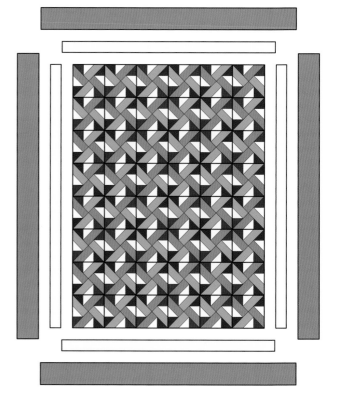

Quilt assembly

Finishing the Quilt

For detailed instructions on the following techniques, refer to "Finishing Techniques" on page 75.

1. Mark the quilting lines, if desired. Layer the quilt top with batting and backing; baste.
2. Hand or machine quilt. Follow the quilting suggestion shown at right or use your own design.
3. Prepare the 2¼"-wide binding strips and sew the binding to the quilt.
4. Add a hanging sleeve if desired. Sign and date your quilt.

Quilting diagram

Midnight Madness

Pieced by Gayle Bong and quilted by Judy Johnson

*The wonderful combination of a pink floral and coordinating
pink, gold, and green prints make this a soft, romantic quilt.*

Materials

Yardage is based on 42"-wide fabric.
4½ yards of pink floral fabric for blocks,
    border, and binding
3¼ yards *total* of assorted medium and dark prints
    in pink, gold, and green for blocks
2½ yards of cream fabric for background
8½ yards of fabric for backing*
93" x 93" piece of batting
See page 75 for backing options.

Cutting

Please read all the directions before starting.
From the assorted medium and dark prints, cut a
total of:
60 strips, 3⅜" x 20"

From the pink floral fabric, cut:
6 strips, 11¼" x 42"
9 border strips, 6½" x 42"
9 binding strips, 2¼" x 42"

From the cream background fabric, cut:
6 strips, 11¼" x 42"
36 squares, 3⅜" x 3⅜"; cut once diagonally to yield
    72 half-square triangles

Making the Blocks

After sewing each seam, press the seam allowances in the direction indicated by the arrows.

1. Place the medium or dark strips right sides
    together with the *beginning* ends staggered

about 10". Sew the strips together along both
long edges to make a strip set. For detailed
instructions see "Scrap Combinations" on page
13. Cut 144 squares, 3⅜" each, trimming and
discarding any section that spans a seam. Cut
each square once diagonally, alternating the
direction of each diagonal cut as shown. Make
288 Twin Peaks units.

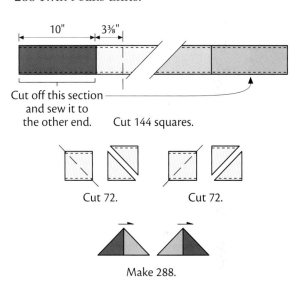

Cut 144 squares.

Cut 72.   Cut 72.

Make 288.

2. Sew two Twin Peaks units together to make an
    hourglass unit. Refer to "Pressing" on page 16
    to press the seam allowances in a pinwheel
    fashion so that they will oppose when sewing
    the units together. Make 144 units.

Make 144.

3. Sew four hourglass units together. Sew a cream triangle to each end of the row. Repeat to make 36 center rows.

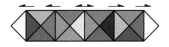

Make 36.

4. Place a cream strip on top of an 11¼" pink floral strip, right sides together and raw edges aligned. Press the strips together. Crosscut the strips into 18 pairs of squares, 11¼" each. Without disturbing the squares, cut each pair of cream/pink squares twice diagonally to make pairs of quarter-square triangles ready to sew. With the cream triangle on top, sew the triangles together starting at the square end. Make 72 units.

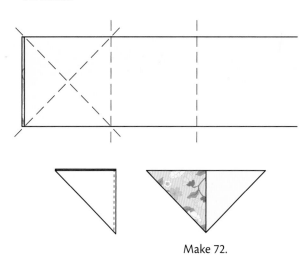

Make 72.

Bias Edge Pressing Tip

To avoid stretching the long bias edge of the pink and cream triangles, do not press the seam allowance until after the next step. Instead, finger-press the end of the seam allowance that will be stitched to the center row.

5. Sew triangle units from step 4 to each side of a center row from step 3 to make a block. Make 36 blocks.

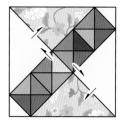

Make 36.

Quilt Assembly and Borders

1. Arrange the blocks in six rows of six blocks each, rotate every other block 90° as shown in the quilt assembly diagram below. Sew the blocks into rows, and then sew the rows together; press.
2. Refer to "Borders" on page 17 to measure, cut, and sew the 6½"-wide pink floral strips to the quilt top for the outer border.

Quilt assembly

Finishing the Quilt

For detailed instructions on the following techniques, refer to "Finishing Techniques" on page 75.

1. Mark the quilting lines, if desired. Layer the quilt top with batting and backing; baste.
2. Hand or machine quilt. Follow the quilting suggestion shown at right or use your own design.
3. Prepare the 2¼"-wide binding strips and sew the binding to the quilt.
4. Add a hanging sleeve if desired. Sign and date your quilt.

Quilting diagram

Steps to Piece

Pieced and quilted by Gayle Bong

Finished Quilt: 44⅝" x 57¾"

Tumbling blocks look great in a variety of fabrics, and this version is particularly appealing because set-in pieces are not required! You could use scraps or novelty prints for the light squares, or choose Asian-themed fabrics, just to name a few possibilities.

Materials

Yardage is based on 42"-wide fabric.

2 yards of brown fabric for blocks, border, and binding

¾ yard *each* of light green, light pink and light gold fabrics for plain squares and side triangles*

⅜ yard *each* of medium green, medium pink and medium gold fabrics for blocks

3 yards of fabric for backing**

50" x 63" piece of batting

To make the quilt as shown in the photo on page 66, you'll need two light green, two light pink, and two light gold prints.

**See page 75 for backing options.*

Cutting

Please read all the directions before starting.

From *each* medium green, medium pink and medium gold fabric, cut:

2 strips, 3½" x 42"; crosscut *each* strip into
- 2 strips, 3½" x 36" (6 total)
- 2 squares, 3½" x 3½" (6 total); cut once diagonally to make 12 half-square triangles

From the brown fabric, cut:

5 border strips, 5½" x 42"

6 strips, 3½" x 42"; crosscut into
- 6 strips, 3½" x 36"
- 5 squares, 3½" x 3½"; cut once diagonally to make 10 half-square triangles (You'll have one extra triangle.)

6 binding strips, 2¼" x 42"

From *each* light green, light pink and light gold fabric, cut:

3 strips, 4½" x 42"; crosscut into 18 squares, 4½" x 4½" (54 total)

1 square, 6½" x 6½"; cut twice diagonally to make 4 quarter-square triangles (12 total)

Making the Blocks

After sewing each seam, press the seam allowances in the direction indicated by the arrows.

1. Place a 36"-long medium green strip on top of a 36"-long brown strip, right sides together, and sew the strips together along *both* long edges as shown. Refer to "Basic Twin Peaks Construction" on page 11 for details. Repeat to sew medium pink strips and brown strips together, and then medium gold strips and brown strips together. Make two of each combination of fabrics. Making sure the green, pink, or gold prints are on top, cut 18 squares from each combination of fabrics, 3½" each. Cut each square once diagonally to make 36 Twin Peaks units for each combination of fabrics, cutting all diagonals in the same direction as shown.

Make 2 strip sets of each color combination.
Cut 9 squares from each strip set.

Cut all squares at this angle.

Make 36 of each.

2. Sew a light green quarter-square triangle to a green/brown Twin Peaks unit as shown to make a triangle end unit. Make four green triangle end units. Repeat to make two pink and three gold triangle end units. You'll have two extra pink quarter-square triangles and one extra gold quarter-square triangle for your scrap box.

Make 4.   Make 2.   Make 3.

3. Sew together one light green square, one green/brown Twin Peaks unit, one brown triangle, and one medium green triangle to make a square end unit as shown. Make four green square end units. Repeat to make two pink and three gold square end units. You'll have two extra pink half-square triangles and one extra gold half-square triangle for your scrap box.

Make 4.   Make 2.   Make 3.

4. Sew Twin Peaks units to opposite sides of each square from the same color family as shown to make parallelogram units. Make 14 green, 16 pink, and 15 gold units.

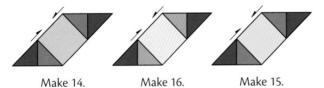

Make 14.   Make 16.   Make 15.

Quilt Assembly and Borders

1. Arrange and sew the pieces in rows as shown in the quilt assembly diagram; press. Sew the rows together; press the seam allowances in one direction.

2. Refer to "Borders" on page 17 to measure, cut, and sew the 5½"-wide brown strips to the quilt top for the outer border.

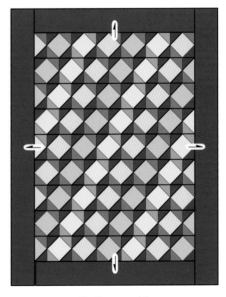

Quilt assembly

Finishing the Quilt

For detailed instructions on the following techniques, refer to "Finishing Techniques" on page 75.

1. Mark the quilting lines, if desired. Layer the quilt top with batting and backing; baste.
2. Hand or machine quilt. Follow the quilting suggestion shown at right or use your own design.
3. Prepare the 2¼"-wide binding strips and sew the binding to the quilt.
4. Add a hanging sleeve if desired. Sign and date your quilt.

Quilting diagram

Flying Geese Incorporated

Pieced and quilted by Gayle Bong

I composed this quilt on my flannel wall just by playing with the triangle units. A close look at the rickrack border reveals Flying Geese units opposite Twin Peaks units.

Materials

Yardage is based on 42"- wide fabric.
1¼ yards *total* of assorted medium and dark prints for the blocks
¾ yard of cream fabric for background
⅝ yard of light yellow fabric for background
1 yard of green fabric for border and binding
3 yards of fabric for backing*
49" x 49" piece of batting
See page 75 for backing options.

Cutting

Please read all the directions before starting.
From the assorted medium and dark prints, cut:
22 strips, 3½" x 20"; crosscut *each* strip into
- 1 strip, 3½" x 16" (22 total)
- 1 square, 3½" x 3½" (22 total); cut once diagonally to yield 44 half-square triangles

From the cream background fabric, cut:
2 strips, 6½" x 42"; crosscut into 9 squares, 6½" x 6½". Cut twice diagonally to yield 36 quarter-square triangles.
2 squares, 9⅛" x 9⅛"; cut twice diagonally to yield 8 quarter-square triangles. Trim the top from each triangle to make trapezoids 3⅛" tall.

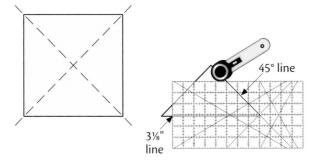

3⅛" line

45° line

From the light yellow background fabric, cut:
2 squares, 11¾" x 11¾"; cut twice diagonally to yield 8 quarter-square triangles
2 squares, 6½" x 6½"; cut twice diagonally to yield 8 quarter-square triangles

From the green fabric, cut:
4 border strips, 3½" x 42"
5 binding strips, 2¼" x 42"

Making the Blocks

After sewing each seam, press the seam allowances in the direction indicated by the arrows.

1. Place two medium or dark strips right sides together, with the ends staggered about 8". Sew the strips together along *both* long edges to make a strip set. For detailed instructions see "Scrap Combinations" on page 13. Press to set the seams. Cut 42 squares, 3½" each, trimming and discarding any section that spans a seam. Cut each square once diagonally, alternating the direction of each diagonal cut as shown. Make 84 Twin Peaks units.

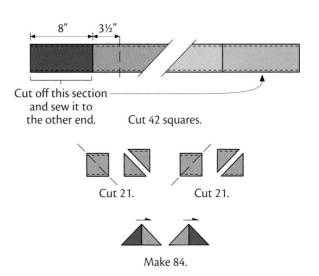

8" 3½"

Cut off this section and sew it to the other end.   Cut 42 squares.

Cut 21.   Cut 21.

Make 84.

2. Sew a Twin Peaks unit to a 6½" cream triangle as shown. Make 20. Sew a Twin Peaks unit to each 6½" yellow triangle. Make eight.

Make 20. Make 8.

3. Sew a Twin Peaks unit to adjacent sides of each unit from step 2. Make 20 cream units and eight yellow units.

Make 20. Make 8.

4. Sew two cream units and two yellow units together as shown to make a block. Make four blocks. (You'll have 12 cream units left to use in "Making the Borders.")

 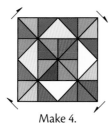

Make 4.

Making the Borders

1. Sew an 11¾" yellow triangle to adjacent sides of a cream triangle unit. Refer to "Trimming Points" on page 15 to use a trimming template to help align the triangles for sewing. Press the seam allowances toward the yellow triangles. Make four side units.

Make 4.

2. Sew remaining cream triangle units together in pairs as shown to make corner units. Press the seam allowances open. Make four corner units.

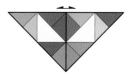

Make 4.

3. Sew medium or dark triangles to adjacent sides of each remaining 6½" cream triangle; press. Make 16 border units.

Make 16.

4. Sew a medium or dark triangle to one end of each cream trapezoid as shown to make end units; press. Make four with the triangle on the right side and four with the triangle on the left side. (You'll have four medium or dark triangles left for your scrap box.)

Make 4 of each.

5. Sew four border units from step 3 and two end units from step 4 together as shown to make a border strip. Press the seam allowances open. Make four.

Make 4.

Quilt Assembly and Borders

1. Sew the four blocks together, then add the side units, and finally sew the corner units. Press the seam allowance toward the side units.

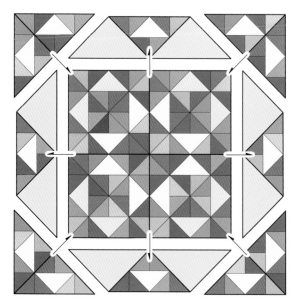

2. Pin the pieced border strips to the quilt, matching centers, quarter points, and ends. Sew the borders to the quilt, easing to fit, and begin and end your stitching ¼" from each corner. (This will allow for the mitered corner.) Backstitch to secure the seams. Sew the diagonal seam in the corner, keeping the seam allowance free. Press the seam allowances open.

3. Measure the length and width of the quilt top through the center. If the measurements differ, calculate the average and use that measurement as the length for each side; then add 3". (Mathematically it should be 40¼".) Trim each 3½"-wide green strip to fit your measurement. You'll be sewing the outer-border strips to the quilt top in a counterclockwise direction using a partial seam. Pin and sew a border strip to one side, leaving about 6" open at one end as shown. Add the remaining border strips. After the last strip is added, sew the open section of the border seam closed. Press all seam allowances toward the newly added border strips.

Quilt assembly

Finishing the Quilt

For detailed instructions on the following techniques, refer to "Finishing Techniques" on page 75.

1. Mark the quilting lines, if desired. Layer the quilt top with batting and backing; baste.
2. Hand or machine quilt. Follow the quilting suggestion shown at right or use your own design.
3. Prepare the 2¼"-wide binding strips and sew the binding to the quilt.
4. Add a hanging sleeve if desired. Sign and date your quilt.

Quilting diagram

Finishing Techniques

I often say the quilt is finished when the top is done. I like to leave a quilt top "as is" until I need it quilted. Maybe this is a luxury of having so many quilts. I can display a quilt top, sell it, finish it as a summer quilt, make it into a jacket, or use it to back another quilt, as I did in "Rust Spots" on page 40. I imagine you'll want to finish your quilt top to use as a quilt, so following are instructions for my finishing methods.

Quilt Backs

The project instructions indicate yardage required for backs based on 42"-wide fabric. All backs are made 4" to 6" larger than the finished quilt top. This extra is necessary to allow for slight shifting of the layers and the natural shrinkage that occurs when layers are quilted. For all of the quilts in this book, you will need to stitch two or more pieces of fabric together to make the backing. You can place the seams anywhere you want. I prefer to use a ½" seam allowance. Remove the selvages before sewing the pieces together. Press the seam allowances open to make quilting the top easier.

When the fabric I have on hand is a little narrower than what I need for a quilt back, I add a strip to make the back the desired size. Sometimes I cut and piece leftover fabric from the front of the quilt and sew it into a strip the width I need to make the backing wider. Other times I piece the backs in the simplest of patterns using coordinating fabric from my stash. If you have a stash that needs thinning, consider piecing your quilt backs.

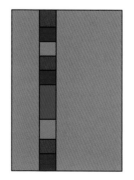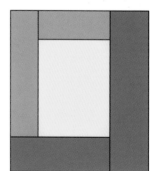

Simple pieced quilt backs

75

For bed-sized quilts, it may be more economical to use extra-wide backing fabric. You will need to determine the fabric requirements if you choose this route.

If you plan to take your quilt top to a professional long-arm quilter, the backing may need to be larger than directed in this book. Check with the quilter before preparing your finished quilt top and backing to determine the correct size of backing needed, and leave layering to the professional quilter.

Basting

You will need a large, flat surface for basting your quilt. To begin, use masking tape to secure the backing wrong side up on a flat surface, taking care not to stretch the fabric out of shape. Spread and smooth the batting over the backing. Then center the quilt top, right side up, over the batting, making sure that all layers stay smooth and even. Make long basting stitches in horizontal and vertical rows 4" apart if you will be hand quilting. Pin baste every 4", if you will be machine quilting. Avoid placing pins in areas where you intend to quilt.

Basting Pins

When pin basting, insert the safety pins and leave them open. When the entire quilt top is basted, first remove the tape holding the back in place, and then close the pins. With less tension on the fabric the pins will be easier to close.

Quilting

As much as I love the relaxing pace of hand quilting, my passion for producing quilt tops is greater. As a result, all the quilts in this book were machine quilted, some by me and others by professional long-arm quilters. Many of my first quilts were just quilted in the ditch along seam lines. Free-motion quilting didn't come naturally to me as it does to some quilters. But with practice, I could do it too.

I like to machine quilt using cotton thread that matches the quilt top. First, I do straight-line quilting, or I quilt in the ditch along the seams between blocks. For this type of quilting, it is extremely helpful to have a walking foot to help feed the three quilt layers through the machine so they don't shift or pucker. Free-motion or curved quilting designs are then added using a darning foot with the feed dogs dropped or covered. Try different threads, needles, and machine tension to see what works best with the fabric and batting you have chosen. Experimenting with identical scraps is a good warm-up exercise and is also great for practicing new quilting designs. The goal is smooth lines in the design with consistently sized stitches and even tension.

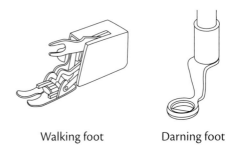

Walking foot   Darning foot

Many excellent books are available to help you perfect your quilting skills, but if at all possible, I suggest you take a class. Not only are they inspirational and more fun than teaching yourself, but they provide the opportunity to learn from the experience of others.

Binding

After completing the quilting, machine baste in the seam allowance along all four edges of the quilt. Trim the batting and backing even with the top and bind the quilt following these steps.

1. Referring to the cutting instructions for the quilt you're making, cut the number of 2¼"-wide strips required to bind the quilt. Cut each end of each strip at the same 45° angle. Join all the strips end to end and press the seam allowances open. Fold and press the binding in half lengthwise, wrong sides together.

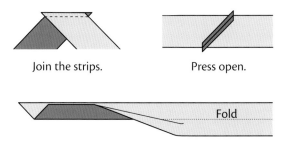

Join the strips.   Press open.

Fold lengthwise and press.

2. Place the beginning of the strip about 20" from the corner of the quilt. Using a ¼" seam allowance, start stitching about 6" from the beginning of the binding. Sew through both layers of the binding and all three layers of the quilt. Keep the edges of the binding even with the edge of the quilt top. Stop stitching ¼" from the corner of the quilt and backstitch. Remove the quilt from under the presser foot.

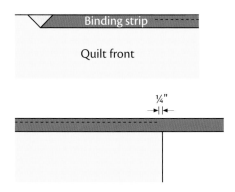

3. Turn the quilt so you can attach the binding to the adjacent edge of the quilt. Fold the binding up at a 90° angle so the fold makes a 45° angle, and then fold the strip down to form a pleat, placing the second fold even with the edge of

the quilt. Keep the raw edges of the binding and the quilt top even. Begin stitching again on the other side of the pleat, ¼" from the edge and continue to ¼" from the next corner. Repeat these steps until all corners are sewn.

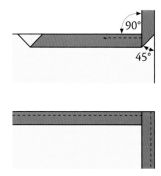

4. Stop stitching about 8" from where you started and backstitch. Remove the quilt from the machine. Unfold the binding and overlap the ends with the beginning tail on top of the end. Mark a diagonal line on the end tail even with the edge of the beginning tail. Make a second mark ½" from the first mark as shown. Cut the binding end at a 45° angle, cutting on the second mark.

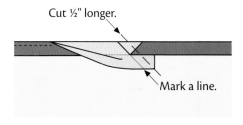

Cut ½" longer.

Mark a line.

5. Sew the two ends right sides together using a ¼" seam allowance. Finger-press the seam allowance open. Refold the binding and finish stitching it in place.

6. Turn the folded edge of the binding to the back of the quilt so it covers the row of machine stitching. Stitch the binding in place with thread that matches the binding. At each

corner, fold the binding to form a miter and hand stitch the miter closed. If I quilted by hand, I sew the binding down by hand with a blindstitch; if I quilted by machine, I sew the binding down by machine. To bind by machine, place the quilt right side up and use an open-toe presser foot with thread that matches the outer border (or clear thread) on top and thread that matches the binding in the bobbin. Stitch in the ditch directly over the seam line catching the binding on the back.

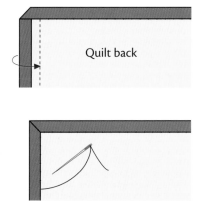

Displaying your Quilts

Quilts covering the walls will add warmth and character to your home. Okay, maybe one quilt will do. Just because I have them in every room in my home doesn't mean you have to. If you choose to hang a quilt, there are several options. Quilt hangers are available that grip the edge of the quilt. The hangers are permanently mounted on the wall. Another option is to hang the quilt from a curtain rod in a pocket or sleeve attached to the back of the quilt. I add sleeves after the quilt has been bound. Following is my method for making sleeves.

1. Cut a strip of fabric as long as the width of your quilt and 9" wide. This will make a 4"-wide sleeve. To make a deeper sleeve, double the desired finished width and add 1" for seam allowances. If, for example, you wish to add a 5"-wide sleeve, cut the fabric strip 11" wide. If you plan to enter your quilt in a show, check the specifications for attaching a sleeve. A 4"-wide sleeve is often required, but standards may differ from one quilt show to another.

2. On each short end of the strip, fold over ½", and then fold ½" again to make a hem. Press and stitch by machine. Fold the strip in half lengthwise, wrong sides together, raw edges aligned and press.

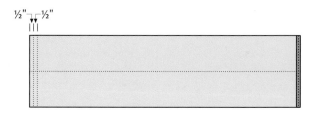

3. Place the sleeve on the back of the quilt so that the folded edge extends beyond the front of the quilt and the raw edges of the sleeve are 1" below the binding. With the quilt right side up and using thread that matches the outer border, machine stitch in the ditch between the binding and border.

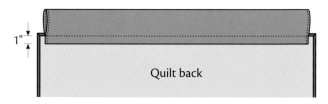

4. Pin the folded edge of the sleeve to the back of the quilt, pushing the edge up about ¼" to allow a little extra room for the hanging rod. This will help the front of the quilt to hang smoothly. Blindstitch the sleeve to the back of the quilt, being careful to only sew through the batting and backing.

Signing the Quilt

Years from now you may wish you remembered when you made a particular quilt, or maybe you won't even be around to say, "I made that quilt." You and your descendants will be pleased if you at least sign and date your quilt. You can use a permanent fabric-marking pen (directly on the back of the quilt if you like) or use fancy embroidery on a special label attached to the back. As many details as desired can be included, such as, city and state, name of the gift recipient and the occasion, and so on. Occasionally I like to machine quilt my name and date into the quilt.

About the Author

Gayle Bong has been an avid quiltmaker for 25 years. She first learned to sew by watching her mother, and by ninth grade she was making most of her own clothes. Designing quilts and writing patterns come naturally to Gayle, who has always been attracted to geometric patterns, fabric, math, puzzles, and writing. She is particularly passionate about her fast, contemporary cutting and piecing techniques and shares them enthusiastically in her classes. This is Gayle's seventh book on quiltmaking.

New and Bestselling Titles from

APPLIQUÉ
Appliqué Quilt Revival—*NEW!*
Beautiful Blooms
Cutting-Garden Quilts
More Fabulous Flowers—*NEW!*
Sunbonnet Sue and Scottie Too

BABIES AND CHILDREN
Baby Wraps
Lickety-Split Quilts for Little Ones
The Little Box of Baby Quilts
Snuggle-and-Learn Quilts for Kids—*NEW!*
Sweet and Simple Baby Quilts

BEGINNER
Color for the Terrified Quilter
Happy Endings, Revised Edition
Let's Quilt!
Machine Appliqué for the Terrified Quilter
Your First Quilt Book (or it should be!)

GENERAL QUILTMAKING
Adventures in Circles—*NEW!*
Bits and Pieces
Charmed
Cool Girls Quilt
Country-Fresh Quilts—*NEW!*
Creating Your Perfect Quilting Space
Creative Quilt Collection Volume Three
A Dozen Roses
Follow-the-Line Quilting Designs
     Volume Three
Gathered from the Garden—*NEW!*
Points of View
Positively Postcards
Prairie Children and Their Quilts
Quilt Revival
A Quilter's Diary
Quilter's Happy Hour
Simple Seasons
Skinny Quilts and Table Runners
Twice Quilted
Young at Heart Quilts

HOLIDAY AND SEASONAL
Christmas with Artful Offerings
Christmas Quilts from Hopscotch—*NEW!*
Comfort and Joy
Holiday Wrappings—*NEW!*

HOOKED RUGS, NEEDLE FELTING, AND PUNCHNEEDLE
The Americana Collection
Miniature Punchneedle Embroidery
Needle-Felting Magic
Needle Felting with Cotton and Wool
Punchneedle Fun

PAPER PIECING
300 Paper-Pieced Quilt Blocks
A Year of Paper Piecing—*NEW!*
Paper-Pieced Mini Quilts
Show Me How to Paper Piece
Showstopping Quilts to Foundation Piece

PIECING
Copy Cat Quilts
Maple Leaf Quilts
Mosaic Picture Quilts
New Cuts for New Quilts
Nine by Nine
On-Point Quilts—*NEW!*
Ribbon Star Quilts
Rolling Along
Quiltastic Curves
Sew One and You're Done
Square Deal
Sudoku Quilts

QUICK QUILTS
40 Fabulous Quick-Cut Quilts
Instant Bargello—*NEW!*
Quilts on the Double
Sew Fun, So Colorful Quilts
Wonder Blocks

SCRAP QUILTS
Nickel Quilts
Save the Scraps
Simple Strategies for Scrap Quilts
Spotlight on Scraps

CRAFTS
Art from the Heart
The Beader's Handbook
Card Design
Creative Embellishments
Crochet for Beaders
Dolly Mama Beads—*NEW!*
Friendship Bracelets All Grown Up—*NEW!*
It's a Wrap
The Little Box of Beaded Bracelets
     and Earrings
Sculpted Threads
Sew Sentimental

KNITTING & CROCHET
365 Crochet Stitches a Year:
     Perpetual Calendar
365 Knitting Stitches a Year:
     Perpetual Calendar
A to Z of Knitting
Amigurumi World
Cable Confidence
Casual, Elegant Knits—*NEW!*
Chic Knits
Crocheted Pursenalities
First Knits
Gigi Knits…and Purls—*NEW!*
Kitty Knits
The Knitter's Book of Finishing Techniques
Knitting Circles around Socks
Knitting with Gigi
Modern Classics
More Sensational Knitted Socks
Pursenalities
Simple Gifts for Dog Lovers
Skein for Skein—*NEW!*

Our books are available at bookstores and your favorite craft, fabric, and yarn retailers. If you don't see the title you're looking for, visit us at www.martingale-pub.com or contact us at:

1-800-426-3126
International: 1-425-483-3313
Fax: 1-425-486-7596 • Email: info@martingale-pub.com